LARGE PRINT

TIRUPATI
BALAJI

OM
Om Books International

Narada's Master Plan

Lord Vishnu had finished his Krishna avtar and returned to Vaikuntha—his heavenly abode. There was tremendous unrest on Earth. Lord Brahma was worried about when Lord

Vishnu would take his next form. He was in serious discussions with the holy sages in his abode, when sage Narada arrived chanting the name of Lord Vishnu. "Narayana! Narayana!" said Narada. "Your presence comforts me Narada. Though you are known

for creating trouble in the three worlds, it always has a good outcome," said Brahma.

"What is your command father?" asked Narada. "I have no command for you, my son. I am only concerned that without Lord Vishnu's presence, the Earth will suffer." "If that is so, I will try and find a way," replied Narada and left.

Narada left his father's heavenly abode and descended to Earth. He walked by the banks of the river Ganga, and found Sage Kashyapa and his disciples performing a holy sacrifice. "Have you decided who among the three gods—Brahma, Vishnu or Shiva— will have the honour of receiving the final offering of this sacrifice?" he asked.

Narada knew that it had not been decided and there would be a dispute among them.

Just as he had thought, he found some sages suggesting Brahma, while Vishnu and Shiva's followers suggested their names. "It is indeed a tough decision. I suggest that we request Sage Bhrigu to conduct a test with the three gods, and decide who the honour should go to," said Narada. Everyone readily agreed. Narada knew that Sage Bhrigu was very arrogant about his spiritual prowess and powers.

Sage Bhrigu was undoubtedly happy about being the chosen one to conduct the test. He began his journey with the first visit to Brahma's abode. He found Brahma in conversation with the sages with Saraswati by his side. Bhrigu stormed into the abode and occupied a seat without even saluting

Brahma. Due to his behaviour, no one paid him any attention. Brahma was offended, and decided to teach Bhrigu a lesson. "Do you consider yourself greater than people like Jamadagni and Anusuya?"

"You are incorrect in your thinking. You could not understand the purpose of my visit to your abode," replied Bhrigu. "Someone as impulsive as you cannot bear the fruit of such a great sacrifice. I curse you that you will

never be worshipped on Earth," said Bhrigu and stormed out.

He went straight to Kailash, the abode of Lord Shiva. He was told by Shiva's attendants that Shiva was busy with his wife, Parvati. Bhrigu did not give an ear to it and walked straight to where Shiva was. Shiva was aghast with Bhrigu's act. Before he could say anything to

Bhrigu, Parvati requested him to control his anger.

But Bhrigu had made up his mind, that Shiva was also not suitable to receive the final offering of the sacrifice. "Shiva! Even you could not understand the purpose of my visit! I curse you that you will be worshipped only as an idol on Earth," said Bhrigu and walked to Vaikuntha.

He found Lord Vishnu resting on Adisesha, the divine serpent, with Goddess Lakshmi pressing his feet. Bhrigu walked towards him, and without a moment's thought kicked him on the chest. Lakshmi was shocked by this. But Vishnu was his calm self. "I only hope the

ornaments studded with precious jewels did not hurt your foot," said Vishnu calming Bhrigu.

Lord Vishnu had known the purpose of Bhrigu's visit with his divine vision and acted accordingly. He made Bhrigu sit down and washed his feet. While doing so, he skillfully pinched the third eye that Bhrigu had in his right foot, which had made him so arrogant.

Having found the god suitable to receive the final offering of the sacrifice, Bhrigu was a changed man. "Oh Lord Vishnu! I was on a mission to find the god to receive the offering of the great sacrifice Sage Kashyapa is performing. I profusely apologise for the wrong I have committed," said Bhrigu.

"I could understand the hidden purpose behind such an act. I am honoured to be the chosen one," replied Vishnu, promising to descend to Earth to accept the offering. Bhrigu returned a happy man, while Goddess Lakshmi was deeply hurt.

Lord Vishnu went to Earth as promised to receive the offering and retuned to his abode. But there was a turn of events.

"Did you realise my Lord that he kicked you on the chest where I reside?" asked Lakshmi. "He has not only hurt you, but he has disrespected me," she added. "He had a hidden

27

purpose," replied Vishnu. But the goddess was not appeased!

"I will leave for Earth, where I will perform a penance," said Lakshmi and left. Lord Vishnu was alone in his abode. He could not bear the separation and also decided to descend to Earth.

Lord Vishnu and the Chola King

Goddess Lakshmi went to Kaveerpura (known as Kolhapur today in India) to perform her penance. Lord Vishnu chose the Seshadri Hills (known as Seven hills or Tirupati today) for his penance. He found an ant hill and sat inside it for his penance.

Meanwhile, Shiva and Brahma were worried that Lord Vishnu and Lakshmi had deserted the heaven. "We have to inform Goddess Lakshmi that Vishnu has gone in her search to Earth," said Shiva.

Soon they met Lakshmi, and told her how lonely Vishnu had felt without her. "He now resides in the Seshadri hills," said Brahma. "We will assume the form of a cow and calf, and you can be the milkmaid who sells us to the Chola King, whose kingdom the Seshadri hills is in," suggested Shiva.

Lakshmi agreed to the plan and went to the Chola King, disguised as a milkmaid and sold him the cow and calf. "The cow and calf look divine," said the queen and asked for a special cowherd to look after them. But the cow and calf were different from the rest.

When the cowherd would take them to the forest, they would move away from the herd and go straight to the ant hill and give all the milk to Lord Vishnu who was sitting inside it. This continued for a few days.

The Chola queen became suspicious that the cowherd had been stealing the milk. "Find out why we do not get any milk from the cow," ordered the queen. The cowherd followed the cow and saw what it was doing. In his anger, he raised his axe and hit the cow with it.

Suddenly the anthill burst open and Lord Vishnu emerged from it, taking the blow on his head. "His head is bleeding! What have I done!" lamented the cowherd. The blood from Vishnu's head splattered on the cow. The cow ran to the King's palace and mooed loudly. The Chola King rushed out and seeing blood on the cow decided to follow it. He reached the anthill and found the cowherd lying on the ground.

"I will punish whoever has done this to the cowherd," he said. Lord Vishnu emerged from the ant hill again. "A master has to bear the sins of his servant. Your servant was about to kill this cow with his axe because it was giving me milk. For this heinous crime, I curse you to die and become an evil spirit. You will roam around this forest," said Vishnu in deep anger.

The Chola King repented for what had happened. "My Lord! I did not know the truth and reacted. Please forgive me," he begged.

Vishnu took pity on him and said, "You will be reborn as King Akasaraja, and will be blessed with a beautiful daughter called Padmavati. I will marry her and give you salvation."

Lord Srinivasa Meets Vakuladevi

In his third divine avtar, Lord Vishnu had assumed the form of a boar—Varaha avtar. He had saved mother Earth from being hidden under the seas by the evil demon, Hiranyaksha.

All the gods had rejoiced and requested Varahaswamy to stay on Earth. "Mankind needs your divine presence. Will you agree to reside and bless mankind by staying on the Seshadri hills by the banks of the sacred Pushkarini?" asked the gods. Varahaswamy agreed and made his abode in the Seshadri hills.

When many avtars later, Vishnu assumed the form of Krishna, he was blessed with two mothers—Devaki and Yashoda. Yashoda was deeply fond of Krishna and could not bear his separation even for a minute.

When she learnt that Krishna's time on Earth was coming to a close, she went to him and said, "Krishna, you have to promise me that you will give me a chance to serve you in your next birth as well." Krishna promised her, and Yashoda was reborn as Vakulamalika. She was staying in the hill shrine of Varahaswamy, where she devoted all her time to chanting the Lord's divine hymns.

When the wounded Lord Vishnu was roaming the hills trying to find medicine for himself, he heard the chanting of divine hymns. He had found the hill shrine of Varahaswamy. While Vishnu was invited inside by

Varahaswamy, and his wound was attended to by Vakuladevi caringly, he narrated the entire story of how Bhrigu had kicked him on the chest, and Lakshmi had thus deserted him. Vishnu also gave Vakuladevi divine vision into her past, and she realised that she had been Yashoda, to whom Krishna had made a promise.

Finally, Vishnu asked Varahaswamy for some land in the Seshadri hills. "I can give you the land, but at a cost," said Varahaswamy. "I don't have any money as Lakshmi has left me. But

I will make you a deal. Every devotee who comes to see me, will visit your shrine first and make an offering," said Vishnu.

Even today, in Tirupati, all the devotees visit Lord Varahaswamy before they seek Lord Balaji's blessings. "What name shall I call you?" asked Vakuladevi. "Srinivasa," replied Lord Vishnu. And the name stuck! Apart from Srinivasa, Lord Vishnu is also known by many other names, including Venkateshwara, Govinda or Balaji.

Lord Srinivasa Marries Padmavati

As the Lord had predicted, the Chola King was reborn as Akasaraja, the King of Chandragiri. The sage Suka was his advisor and teacher. "All is well with me, except that I have still not been blessed with a child," said Akasaraja to sage Suka.

"Perform a holy sacrifice and you will be blessed with one," replied the sage. Akasaraja found a piece of land to perform the sacrifice and used his golden plough to till the land. The plough hit a hard box. When the King opened the box, he was amazed to see a lovely little girl in a lotus inside the box. "I am indeed blessed with this divine child," he thought to himself and took her home. The girl grew up to be a lovely young girl, and was named Padmavati.

One evening, when Padmavati was walking in her garden, she saw a wild elephant charging towards her. "Help! Help!" she cried.

Before the royal guards could run to her rescue, a handsome, young man riding on a horse came towards her and chased the elephant away. It was Lord Srinivasa. Both the Lord and Padmavati had exchanged glances and fallen in love with each other.

Lord Srinivasa walked towards the shy Padmavati. "No stranger can trespass our

garden," said Padmavati's attendants. "I am not here to trespass. I am in love with this beautiful maiden, and would like to marry her," replied the Lord.

"How can you ask for the hand of the daughter of Queen Dharini Devi and King Akasaraja?" asked Padmavati's attendants angrily. "I am also of a noble descent," replied the Lord. "I am destined to marry only Lord

Srinivasa," said Padmavati quietly. But before the Lord could tell her who she was, the attendants threw stones at him, forcing him to leave. But neither could he forget her nor could Padmavati forget him.

So Srinivasa told Vakuladevi about his love for Padmavati, and asked her to approach Queen Dharini Devi. While Vakuladevi proceeded for

Chandragiri, the Lord disguised himself as a brahmin and met Queen Dharini Devi as a fortune teller. "Your daughter is in love with the Lord himself. An old lady will come here seeking her hand. Accept the proposal," said Lord Srinivasa in the form of the brahmin to the queen.

Vakuladevi reached the palace and sought the hand of Padmavati for Srinivasa. After consulting sage Suka and King Akasaraja, Queen Dharini Devi accepted the proposal.

The stage was finally set for the divine wedding!

But the Lord was worried. "How will I bear the expenses of the wedding?" he asked Lord

Shiva. "After Lakshmi deserted me, I am left with no money," he said. So they decided to approach Kubera, the god of wealth. Kubera gladly gave Lord Srinivasa the money, on the condition that he would pay it back during Kali yuga (the present era). It was indeed a divine wedding, with all the gods, goddesses and sages descending to Earth for it. Goddess Lakshmi came for the wedding from Kaveerpura.

The couple lived happily, but not for too long. Padmavati received the news that her father, King Akasaraja was very ill. Soon he passed away, and there was a dispute between his son Vasudaman and his brother,

Thondaman for the throne. Lord Srinivasa tried resolving it, but both of them took to a fight.

Unfortunately, Thondaman shot an arrow that hit the Lord on his chest, and he became

unconscious. When Vasudaman and Thondaman saw the Lord injured, they repented and begged for forgiveness. "The kingdom will be equally shared between the two of you. I will reside here with Padmavati. Thondaman! You will have to build a shrine for us," said the Lord.

And thus, Ananda Nilayam was built. But the Lord needed Goddess Lakshmi to return to him. "Lakshmi, please return to Ananda Nilayam and bless all the devotees who visit the shrine. I will thus be able to return the loan I have taken from Kubera," said the Lord. Sage Bhrigu, who had angered Goddess Lakshmi, apologised to her. "I will come to Ananda Nilayam and live in the Padma Sarovar," said Goddess Lakshmi.

And, thus was built Tirupati, on the seven hills, where Lord Srinivasa, Padmavati and Goddess Lakshmi reside, and bless every